D0503089

ART CENTER COLLEGE OF DESIGN

3 3220 00307 0039

BEST ADS SHOCK IN ADVERTISING

DISCARD

SMIRNOFF THE OTHER SIDE.

Smirnoff (A) Lowe Howard-Spink, London
(AD) Brian Campbell (CW) Paul Fella
(P) John Crane (Typographer) Jaz Garcha

Art Center College of Design
Library
1700 Lida Street
Pasadena, Calif. 91103

Benetton (A) In-house, Italy (AD) Oliviero
Toscani (P) Lucinda Devlin

BEST ADS SHOCK IN ADVERTISING

Dave Saunders

B.T. Batsford Ltd, London

To my kids, who will have to cope with future shocks

© **Dave Saunders**
First published 1996
All rights reserved. No part of this publication may be reproduced in any form or by any means without permission from the Publisher.

Printed in Singapore

for the publishers

B.T. Batsford Ltd
4 Fitzhardinge Street
London W1H 0AH

ISBN 0 7134 7904 3

A CIP catalogue record for this book is available from the British Library.

(A) Agency, (CD) Creative Director, (AD) Art Director, (CW) Copywriter, (P) Photographer, (M) Model

CONTENTS

Art Center College of Design
Library
1700 Lida Street
Pasadena, Calif. 91103

Has the spirit of Doyle Dane Bernbach's disarming Volkswagen ('folk car') advertising of the 1960s returned to undermine the consumer gloss of the 1980s and re-invigorate the ad industry of the nineties?

Early Volkswagen ads revolutionized advertising. Bill Bernbach in New York decided to advertise the VW Beetle for what it was, rather than to hype it up beyond credibility. It was the opposite to aspirational advertising ... engagingly honest and talking to the reader as an intelligent friend.

Had the VW Beetle been a normal car, it wouldn't have worked. The car may have been designed by Porsche, but it was ugly, small and had an engine in the back. 'Lemon' and 'Ugly is only skin deep' were two of the very early headlines. Refreshing antidotes to the American dream, and people quickly grew to love the ugly little lemon.

How far have we travelled since then? And what have we learned?

AGITATE
APPAL
ASTOUND
CONFOUND
DISGUST
DISMAY
DISQUIET
HORRIFY
JAR
JOLT
NUMB
OFFEND
OUTRAGE
PARALYSE
REVOLT
SCANDALISE
SHAKE
SICKEN
STAGGER
STUN
STUPEFY
UNNERVE
UNSETTLE
... SHOCK?

Lemon.

This Volkswagen missed the boat.

The chrome strip on the glove compartment is blemished and must be replaced. Chances are you wouldn't have noticed it; Inspector Kurt Kroner did.

There are 3,389 men at our Wolfsburg factory with only one job: to inspect Volkswagens at each stage of production. (3000 Volkswagens are produced daily; there are more inspectors than cars.)

Every shock absorber is tested (spot checking won't do), every windshield is scanned. VWs have been rejected for surface scratches barely visible to the eye.

Final inspection is really something! VW inspectors run each car off the line onto the Funktionsprüfstand (car test stand), tote up 189 check points, gun ahead to the automatic brake stand, and say "no" to one VW out of fifty.

This preoccupation with detail means the VW lasts longer and requires less maintenance, by and large, than other cars. (It also means a used VW depreciates less than any other car.)

We pluck the lemons; you get the plums.

Volkswagen of America
(A) Doyle Dane Bernbach, New York
(AD) Helmut Krone (P) Wingate Paine

Fear

**Samaritans (A) Saatchi & Saatchi, London
(AD) Fergus Fleming (CW) Simon Dicket
(P) Barney Edwards**

It's the nightmare version of Edvard Munch's 'Scream'. Fear of rejection, of solitude, of isolation. Most agencies like to have a few charity accounts. Saatchis more than most. Even though they usually end up costing the agency money, charity ads, or public service announcements, provide great scope for hard-hitting work. Young creative teams cut their teeth on them.

Videofilmes/High Art, Rio de Janeiro
(P) Marcia Ramalho

The shock tactic used by the publicity machine for horror movies is diluted by its predictability. Although the picture is more life-like than the creative interpretation used for the Samaritans ad, we view horror movies as entertainment. We expect them to scare or amuse, rather than evoke genuine cause for concern.

PETER COYOTE
A GRANDE ARTE
(H I G H   A R T)

Do romance de Rubem Fonseca
com TCHEKY KARYO, AMANDA PAYS
RAUL CORTEZ, GIULIA GAM

DOLBY STEREO ®
IN SELECTED THEATRES

Distribuição

**British Telecom (A) Cousins Advertising,
London (AD & CW) Jon Cousins (P) Tom
Mulvee**

Imagine the scenario. It's late. You're
miserable. Missed the bus. Are you
equipped to cope with it? Are you just
frustrated, or is there a more sinister
fear lingering in the dark? The ad taps
into our fears, then offers a solution.

It's late.

You're miserable.

Missed the bus.

Dinner's in your bag.

*You want to phone
home.*

*But your son's
chatting to a friend.*

*So you can't get
through.*

*And you wish
you'd accepted this
free offer.*

With BT Call Waiting, you could have let him
know you needed to get through, and that you
wanted a lift. So how about trying the service
absolutely free of charge for 3 months?

Then, if you ring home when the phone is
already in use, instead of hearing the engaged
signal you'll get a message asking you to hold.

Meanwhile your son (or whoever's using
your phone) will hear a bleep telling him someone
wants to get through.

He can then put his first caller on hold,
speak to you, and finally return to the other person.

Call Waiting is great if you're on the phone
when another important call needs to get through.

To continue with the service after your free
trial period, the rental is just £4 a quarter for at
least nine months – making a minimum total of £12.

Of course if you find it isn't for you, you can
cancel it during this trial period by letting us know.
But before you 'buy', give it a try. To apply,
or for more details, return the coupon or
call us now on **Free***fone* **0800 800 848.**

To use Call Waiting you need a normal tone dialling phone, and to be in one of the many areas with a modern digital BT exchange. All prices include VAT.

Call Waiting
FREE TRIAL OFFER
☐ YES. Please arrange a 3 month rent free trial of Call Waiting.
☐ YES. Please send details of the new BT phone which gives
you access to Call Waiting at the touch of a single button.

Surname: Mr/Mrs/Miss/Ms

Initials   Tel no

Address

Postcode

Please send to: BT Call Waiting Free Offer, FREEPOST
(BS6295), Bristol BS1 2BR. (No stamp required.)

BT

It's good to talk

London Fire Brigade (A) McCann Erickson, London (AD/CW) Toby Talbot/Jeneal Rohrback (P) Snowdon

It can happen to me. Death by fire. Death by neglect. Death by good intentions. Excuses, excuses. It's too late; the barn door has already burned down.

Metropolitan Police (A) Collett Dickenson Pearce, London (AD) Neil Godfrey (CW) Indra Sinha (P) Don McCullin

McCullin did not want his original reportage image of a 'real' tramp to be used in advertising. He reshot the photograph using a heavily made-up model.

HOW WOULD YOU LIKE TO SPEND THE NIGHT WITH HIM?

Police work isn't all cops and robbers. It's also looking after people – and that means everyone. Even those who live underneath the arches. There's no point in moving him on if he has nowhere to go. Why not try talking to him instead? **Photograph by Don McCullin**

MANY TIMES THE EFFECTS OF STRESS DON'T SHOW UP ON THE JOB.

The fact is, stress keeps close to one million people from going to work every day.

For many businesses, it's leading to expensive, long-term disabilities now costing an average of $73,000 each claim.

Even when employees make it to work, stress has become the number-one hazard in the workplace. Three of four employees say they have frequent illness caused by stress.

Let's do something about it.

At Northwestern National Life, our disability programs specialize in the rehabilitation of stress-disabled workers. In fact, we have saved employers $38 for every $1 invested in stress rehabilitation.

To help you better measure the extent of your employees' stress, let us send you our new 1992 research—*Burnout: Causes and Cures.*

For your free copy, call or write Rick Naymark, Northwestern National Life, Box 20, Minneapolis, MN 55440, (612) 342-7137.

We want to help uncover the problems you and your employees may be having with stress.

Northwestern National Life

Northwestern National Life Insurance Company, Minneapolis, MN (not admitted in the state of New York). The North Atlantic Life Insurance Company of America, Jericho, NY (a member of The NWNL Companies, Inc.) Sources of statistics are *Stress in the American Workplace*, LRP Publications, 1989. and *Employee Burnout: America's Newest Epidemic*, NWNL, 1991.

Northwestern National Life (A) Clarity Coverdale Fury, Minneapolis (AD) Jac Coverdale (CW) Jerry Fury (P) Steve Umland

Stress. Compensation comes in handy, but cures are better. It means the insurance company doesn't have to keep shelling out. The ad is saying - as gently as is still effective - 'Get your act together'.

Europeiske Medical Insurance
(A) Saatchi & Saatchi, Oslo
(AD) Kjell Bryngell (CW) Ragnar Dahl
(P) Stein Jørgensen

The ad, generated in Norway, is promoting medical insurance, but it's written in English, so whose health system is the scalpel aimed at? Wouldn't social welfare be a simpler solution?

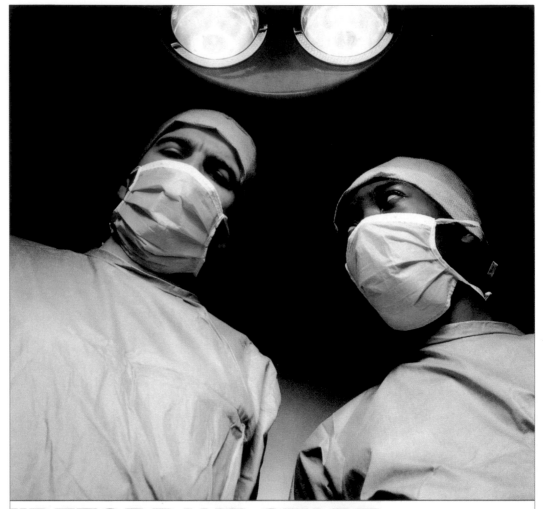

"BEFORE WE START, WHO IS PAYING FOR THIS?"

Hva gjør du?
Du er blitt syk, du er på reise, du trenger hjelp, men du får ikke hjelp.
   Er du vant med norsk helsevesen, vil du møte en ganske annen virkelighet i utlandet: De hjelper så gjerne, men de vil ha garanti for betaling først.
   Et eksempel: En av våre kunder fikk hjerteproblemer på ferie i USA og måtte opereres. Regningen fra sykehuset var kr. 323.500,-
   De færreste har slike reserver med seg på reisen. Da gjelder det å ha firmaets reiseforsikringer i orden. Men visste du at ikke alle forsikringer er like godt kjent i utlandet?
   Konsekvensen er ofte at det blir vanskelig å få den hjelpen du trenger. Europeiske har et nettverk av kontorer og samarbeidspartnere over hele kloden. Også i Sovjet, Kina og USA.
   Det har gjort oss kjent. Derfor kan våre kunder være trygge om et uhell skulle inntreffe. Uansett hvor og når.
   Europeiske gir dessuten mer enn økonomisk hjelp og erstatning.

Du får også praktisk, menneskelig hjelp. Noen som behersker språket, har kjennskap til de lokale forhold og som kjenner prosedyrene i forhold til sykehus, politi og andre. Dette kaller vi aktiv skadehjelp.
   For bedrifter har vi utviklet en egen forsikringsmeny. Kontakt oss, nærmeste Storebrand-kontor eller ditt reisebyrå, så kan du få vite mer om den.
   Med dette kortet er du garantert hjelp over hele verden.

EUROPEISKE
REISEFORSIKRING A/S

Haakon VII's gt. 10, 0161 Oslo 1, Tlf. (02) 31 10 20

STOREBRAND

Commercial Union (A) CME-KHBB, London
(CD) Barbara Nokes (AD) Gary Denham
(CW) Susie Henry (P) Malcolm Venville

Whatever happens, insurance can provide a
safety net. So keep your hair on, and don't
make a drama out of a crisis.

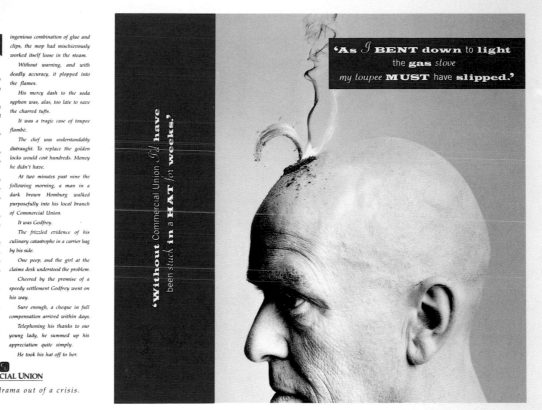

Pain

What sort of pain is it? your doctor asks. Stabbing pain, sawing pain? Thumping, pinching, punching pain? Visualize it. Describe it. Then put them all together in one picture. If you can feel the picture, you'll relate to the ad, and then equate the product with the solution to the pain.

  With Arcimboldo as a guide and expressionist paintings as inspiration, the creative team constructed an abrasive sculpture, which was photographed, then blended, using a Quantel Paintbox.

Crookes Healthcare (A) Gold Greenlees Trott, London (AD) Kate Stanners (CW) Tim Hearn (P) Barney Edwards (Model maker) Assylum (Retouching/handtinting) Dan Tierney

Multiple Sclerosis (A) BMP DDB
Needham, London (AD) Nancy Stephens
(P) Bruce Nicoll

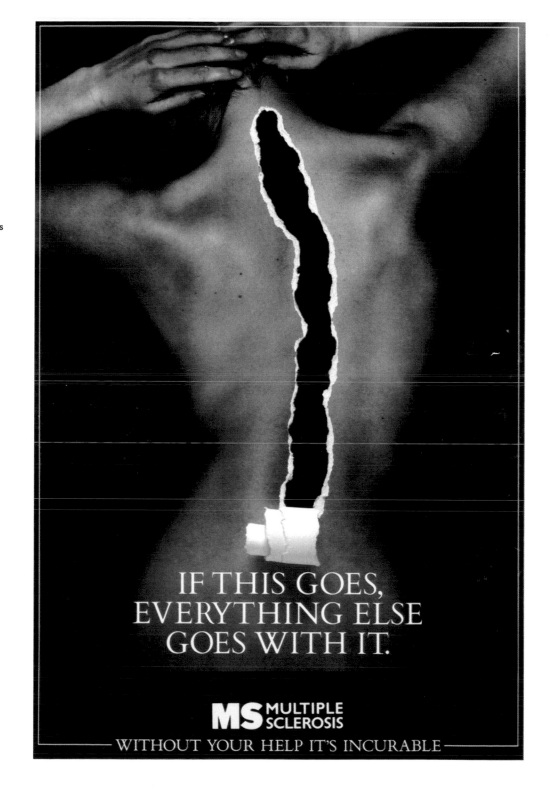

Multiple Sclerosis (A) BMP DDB Needham,
London (AD) Nancy Stephens (P) Bruce Nicoll

Multiple Sclerosis (A) BMP DDB Needham,
London (AD) Mark Reddy (CW) Richard Grisdale
(P) Branka Jukic

She
went swimming
on Monday,
dancing
on Tuesday
and lame
on Wednesday.

MS
MULTIPLE SCLEROSIS
Tears lives apart

IF YOU'D LIKE TO MAKE A DONATION WRITE TO: THE MULTIPLE SCLEROSIS SOCIETY, FREEPOST, 25 EFFIE ROAD, FULHAM, LONDON SW6 1EE. TELEPHONE: 071-736 6267.

People
come to **Putney** from
all over Britain
to improve
their quality of life.

THE ROYAL HOSPITAL AND HOME, PUTNEY
WHERE PEOPLE LEARN TO LIVE, AGAIN.

The Royal Hospital and Home, Putney
(A) J. Walter Thompson, London
(AD) Wayne Pashley (CW) Nigel Pollard
(P) John Claridge

The Putney posters deal with real
lives. Real people with real problems.
Black and white usually means arty or
documentary. Would it work if actors
were used?

AECC Spanish Cancer Association (A) Delvico Bates,
Barcelona (CD) Felix Fernandez de Castro/Toni Segarra
(AD) Enric Aguilera (CW) Toni Segarra (P) Ramon Serrano

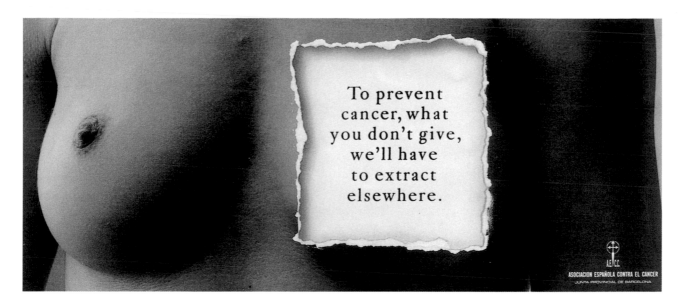

**AECC Spanish Cancer Association (A) Delvico Bates, Barcelona
(CD) Felix Fernandez de Castro/Toni Segarra (AD) Enric Aguilera
(CW) Felix Fernandez de Castro (P) Ramon Serrano**

**AECC Spanish Cancer Association (A) Delvico Bates, Barcelona
(CD) Felix Fernandez de Castro/Toni Segarra (AD) David Caballero
(CW) Pablo Monzon**

To get people to part with their money voluntarily is the driving force behind most advertising. Convince someone of the benefits they will enjoy, and their credit card will be out. But what about charities? What benefits are they giving people? Apart from a feelgood factor, people may be motivated by compassion or guilt or fear. Confront people with different horrors from different viewpoints and you'll twang on a variety of heartstrings - compassion, sympathy, even outrage - each powerful enough to motivate people to action.

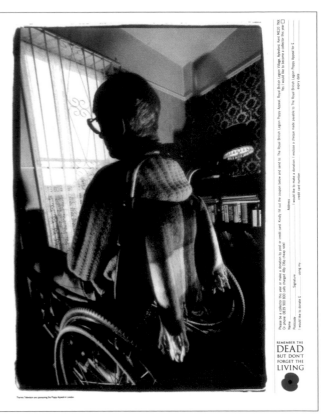

50 YEARS ON THERE ARE STILL PRISONERS OF WAR

They're held captive all over Britain.

In houses with high front steps. Or blocks of high-rise flats.

Today, the lives of many ex-service people are still blighted by the Second World War.

But there is a way out for them.

The Royal British Legion was founded to help all ex-service people and their dependants.

We run residential and convalescent homes where the disabled can be properly looked after. And we provide warden controlled estates where they live securely and comfortably.

We're also the biggest private employer of disabled people in the United Kingdom.

Last year, we managed to help over 100,000 ex-service people and their dependants. But there are still a great many more who need our help.

The Gulf War demonstrates that continuing need.

We're not asking you to give as much as they did. Just as much as you can afford.

This Poppy Day, remember those who can't forget.

Thank you.

REMEMBER THE DEAD BUT DON'T FORGET THE LIVING

Thames Television are sponsoring the Poppy Appeal in London.

Royal British Legion (A) Delaney Fletcher Bozell, London (CD) Brian Stewart (AD) Mark Robinson (CW) Mark Tweddle (P) John Claridge

A rear view and wideangle lens gives it a nightmare quality.
Face silhouetted in the window light, tilted down. You feel
he has been sitting there for all of the 50 years.

Barnardos (A) Maher Bird Associates, London (AD/CW) Stephen Deput/Philip Bird (P) Don McCullin

This campaign, softly echoing John Lennon's plea 'Give peace a chance', attacked child poverty with 96-sheet monochromatic posters. Don McCullin, whose war pictures moved millions, is accustomed to unreasonable behaviour. His own childhood hardships enabled him to empathize with his subjects and, in his own words, 'turn him into a tough little blighter who could stand on his own feet'.

MADE IN BRITAIN

**POVERTY IS A FACT OF LIFE FOR ONE IN FOUR CHILDREN
WE'RE WORKING TO GIVE THEM A DECENT CHILDHOOD**

Barnardos
GIVING CHILDREN A CHANCE

Violence

Benetton (A) In-house, Italy (AD) Oliviero Toscani

Simplistically symbolic. The wires come from South Africa, the former Yugoslavia, Mexico, the Lebanon, Japan, Israel, Hungary, Brazil, Ireland and Germany. Prisons - real or virtual. The campaign appeared in a hundred countries. Benetton opened the door to a new way of using advertising space. The company put one foot over the threshold of a communication revolution but then stayed there, with the door left swinging on its hinges.

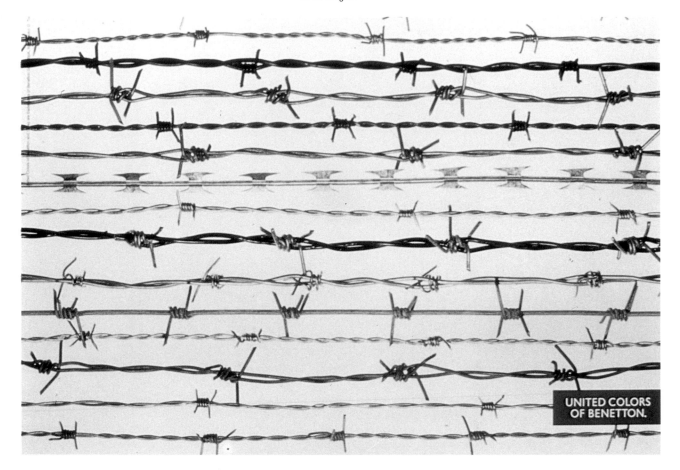

CARRY ONE AND YOU COULD HAVE TWO YEARS TO KILL.

Scottish Office (A) Faulds, Edinburgh (CD) Simon Scott/Andrew Lindsay (AD) Ruth Yee (CW) Ross Thomson (P) Peter Chin

Puns, the fodder of advertising. Why? Do they make us look twice or linger longer? And therefore remember the message? Or do we applaud the cause because we laud the technique?

Following page
Scottish Office (A) Faulds, Edinburgh (AD) Ruth Yee (CW) Craig Jackson (P) Andy Green

Man's inhumanity to Woman. Note that the wedding ring is on the side etched with 'Hate'.

Who is the target market? How will it respond to this punchy ad? While a fist can be used to symbolize Hate, only artistic licence allows it to represent Love.

WHICH ONE WILL YOU

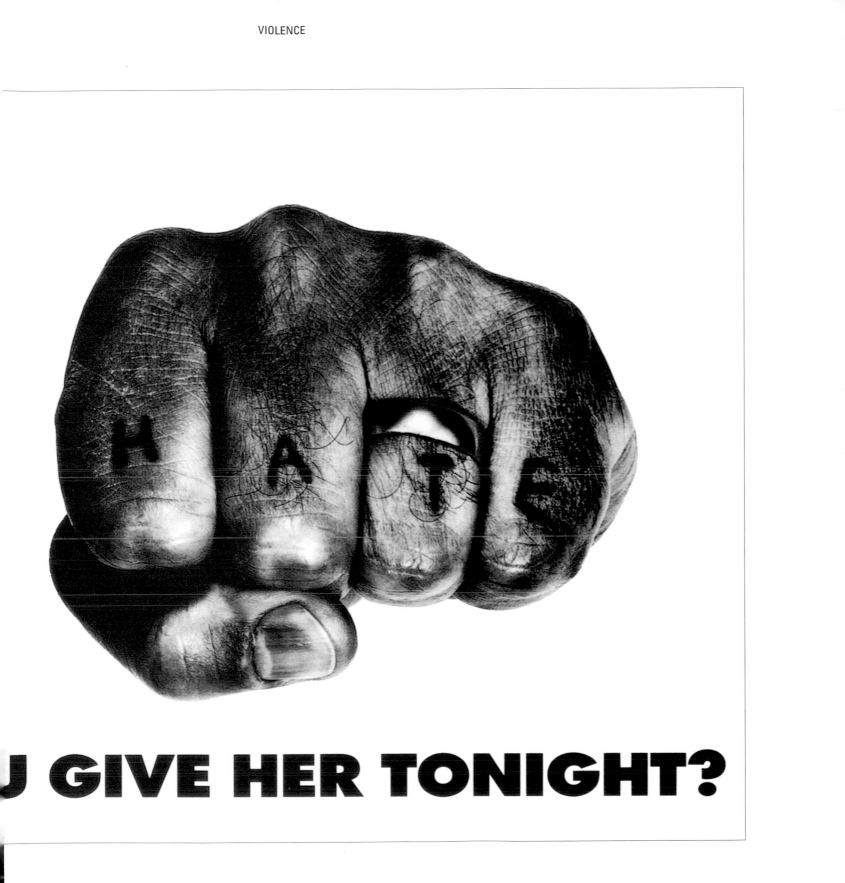

U GIVE HER TONIGHT?

The headline reads: 'Every year 4 million women are beaten in our country'. The normal pose by a normal looking family strikes us like a velvet sledgehammer, inverting the comfortably familiar in order to rattle us out of our complacency.

Jedes Jahr

werden bei uns

4 Millionen Frauen*

mißhandelt.

Fast immer sind es die eigenen Ehemänner oder Lebensgefährten, die Frauen mißhandeln. Körperlich mißhandeln – oft mit alltäglichen Gebrauchsgegenständen und so, daß die Umwelt nichts davon merkt. Seelisch mißhandeln – in vielen Fällen mit ganz bewußt eingesetztem Psychoterror. Gewalt gegen Frauen ist unabhängig vom Bildungs- und Gesellschaftsniveau. Und es ist schwer, die Ausmaße dieser Gewalt zu erfassen. Denn es dauert manchmal viele Jahre, bevor eine mißhandelte Frau über ihre Verletzungen spricht. Hilfe sucht. Gegenmaßnahmen ergreift. Wenn Sie betroffen sind, lassen Sie es nicht so weit kommen. Sprechen Sie mit einer Frauenberatungsstelle in Ihrer Nähe. Oder – rufen Sie uns an. Wir helfen Ihnen.

Frauenberatungsstelle Düsseldorf 02 11/68 68 54.

Women's Counselling Service (A) Grey Düsseldorf, Germany (CDs) Charles Greene/Lindsay Cullen (AD) Marina Lörwald (CW) Tanja Schickert (P) Harry Forsteher

IF THE NOISE COMING

FROM NEXT DOOR

WERE LOUD MUSIC,

YOU'D DO SOMETHING

ABOUT IT.

It's not a private family matter. Every nine seconds another woman is beaten by her husband or boyfriend. And unless we all work together, it's never going to stop. For information about how you can help stop domestic violence, call 1-800-777-1960.

THERE'S **NO** EXCUSE
for Domestic Violence.

**Family Violence Prevention Fund
(A) Hill Holliday/Altschiller, New York
(P) Ken Miller**

Foetal reaction to the released beast.

Washington Humane Society (A) Earle Palmer Brown, Maryland

Did *you* pull the legs off flies? Tie tin cans to cats' tails?
What stops the violence escalating? Can we contain or divert
the violent side of our nature? You don't know until you're tested.
  We believe we're civilized. And society - polite society anyway -
dictates that we don't persecute pets. But society allows us to
swat mosquitoes ... shoot vermin ... splatter jay-walkers. So can
we kill any animal (or person) that threatens us? Or just gets in
our way? Where is the line? Shouting? Smacking? Cracking?

LE WHO ABUSE ANIMALS

RARELY STOP THERE.

that people who abuse their pets are also likely to abuse their kids.
animal mistreated or neglected, please report it. Because the parent
comes home and kicks the cat is probably just warming up.

WASHINGTON HUMANE SOCIETY
202-723-5730

HSUS   FRIENDSHIP HOSPITAL FOR ANIMALS

Sponsored by The Humane Society of the United States and Friendship Hospital for Animals

S4C Halen Yn Gwaed (A) Woollams Moira Gaskin O'Malley, London (AD) Mitch Levy (P) Nick Georghiou

The grimace, the taut clothing, the apparent spray of sweat infuse this image with the desperation of violence. This is a press ad for a TV drama about kidnapping. Art not only imitates life, it serves it up in manageable portions, enabling us to view it with relaxed detachment.

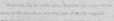

The advertisement headline reads:

The Spanish police didn't like the colour of his skin. So they changed it.

Amnesty International (A) Laing Henry, London (CD) Max Henry (AD) Duncan Marshall (CW) Howard Willmott

Brutality. Have you ever got in touch with those feelings experienced by perpetrators of violence? The sense of justified rage. The driving force that powers those in authority, and is backed by a conviction you're right? Despots have it. Police have it. Playground bullies have it. Parents have it.

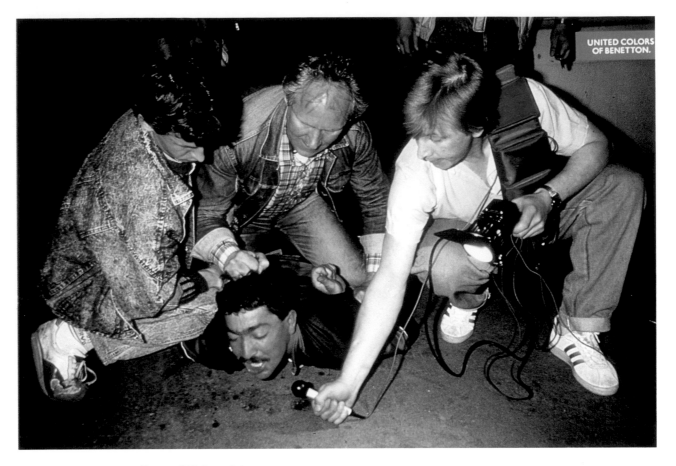

Benetton (A) In-house, Italy
(AD) Oliviero Toscani (P) Hans-Jürgen Burkard

Benetton use documentary images out of context - in a
professed mood of altruism in order to use their advertising
space/budget to bring more important issues to people's
attention. But everybody knows the not-so-hidden agenda
is to cause a stir and push more pullovers.

Amnesty International (A) Doyle Advertising, Boston (AD) John Doyle (CW) Robin Raj (P) Nadav Kander

Her hands are at rest. But the pain is not over. Fatima Ibrahim, a writer, a leader for Sudanese women's rights, was imprisoned when her husband was executed. Denied food and medicine, she fell into a coma. Now released and president of the Women's International Democratic Federation, the pain is not over. And readers are invited to become Freedom Writers for those who can't.

Photographic emphasis is on the hands because of the symbolic as well as real significance of 'hands are tied' and the actual power of hands used for writing.

Art Center College of Design
Library
1700 Lida Street
Pasadena, Calif. 91103

Warnings

Health Education Authority (A) Publicis, London (AD) Rick Ward (CW) Noel Sharman (P) Adrian Burke

Symbolism is poetic shorthand that represents reality in digestible form. But even when packaged with an ambiguous three-way pun, it won't kill smoking. Try Ashes To Ashes.

A QUARTER ᵒꜰ A million PEOPLE PACK it in EVERY YEAR.

Ash Scotland (A) Marr Associates, Edinburgh
(AD) Colin Marr (CW) Tony Veazey (P) Dave
Stewart (Modelmaker) Wesley West

The cigarette end is nigh. Dead end.

**American Lung Cancer (A) Earle Palmer Brown, Maryland
(AD & CW) Taras Wayner**

People are hot on secondary smoking and the invasion of
personal space because you can see the smoke, it gets in your
eyes. It's harder to get people worked up about the rainforest
or the ozone layer because they're several steps removed from
our own immediate perceived space. Or so it seems ...

SUICIDE

MURDER

✝ AMERICAN LUNG ASSOCIATION.
of Maryland, Inc.

© THE AMERICAN LUNG ASSOCIATION OF MARYLAND

Quick.

Slow.

WANT HELP? PHONE THE SMOKELINE ON 0800 84 84 84. YOU CAN DO IT. WE CAN HELP.

Health Education Board for Scotland (A) The Leith Agency, Edinburgh (CD) Jim Downie (AD) Guy Gumm (CW) Gerry Farrell (P) Mike Parsons

It's a great opportunity to be direct and hard-hitting. But which one will stop you in your tracks - the ad or the effect of ignoring the ad?

Simple posters must have immediate impact. Two words. Quick. Slow. Two strong images. Aimed at the target market, which defends itself with smokescreens of platitudes. Yet the subsequent direct response phone calls to the stop-smoking counselling line were more than three times the expected level, based on similar help lines elsewhere (in England and Wales). Six per cent of all smokers in Scotland contacted the Smokeline number within its first year. Based on a sample of the callers, it was estimated that a quarter of respondents were still not smoking a year after contacting Smokeline.

Partnership for a Drug-free America (A) Earle Palmer Brown, Maryland

Anti-cocaine (A) Young & Rubicam, Lisbon

Sharp image. Stark reality. Mess with me kid and you may as well slash your wrists. The stark warning is followed by a smart solution: treatment, explained in English.

Partnership for a Drug-free America (A) Earle Palmer Brown, Maryland

The choice is yours. But is it too patronizing for the users? Condescending in its tone? Will someone, obsessed by his next fix, be jolted into clear-headed reason? Maybe, if they face it early enough.

WE'LL HELP YOU QUIT. JUST TELL US WHICH ONE.

Use drugs, and you're not just harming yourself. You're also hurting your company. Drugs cause on-the-job accidents, putting everyone at risk. They raise health insurance costs. And increase absenteeism, forcing others to cover for you. Ask about your company's employee assistance program, or call 1-800-662-HELP, confidentially. Because it's not your job we want you to lose. It's the drugs.

PARTNERSHIP FOR A DRUG-FREE AMERICA

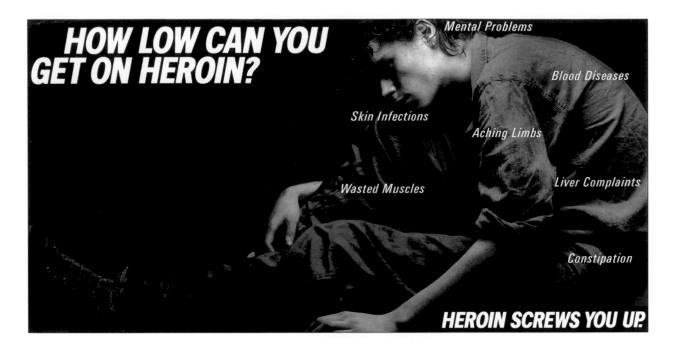

HOW LOW CAN YOU GET ON HEROIN?

Mental Problems

Blood Diseases

Skin Infections

Aching Limbs

Liver Complaints

Wasted Muscles

Constipation

HEROIN SCREWS YOU UP.

Anti-heroin (A) Yellowhammer, London (AD) Jeremy Pemberton (P) Clive Arrowsmith (Make-up) Stephanie Walker

One strong anti-heroin campaign shocked the wrong people! It aimed to show young people the consequences of taking heroin. The subjects had to be believable, yet frightening enough to deter. Models were used rather than real addicts, because of the shortage of volunteers! Skin Care by Heroin ran in women's magazines alongside genuine skin care ads. The unexpected outcome was that the target market identified with, and aspired to, the spotty victims, and started to emulate them.

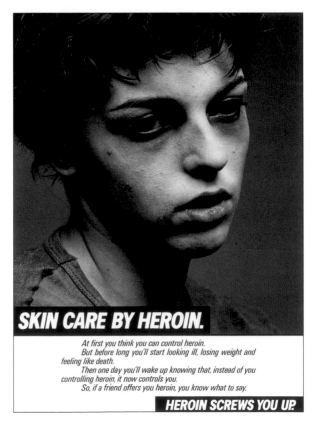

SKIN CARE BY HEROIN.

At first you think you can control heroin.
But before long you'll start looking ill, losing weight and feeling like death.
Then one day you'll wake up knowing that, instead of you controlling heroin, it now controls you.
So, if a friend offers you heroin, you know what to say.

HEROIN SCREWS YOU UP

Partnership for a Drug-free America (A) Hill
Holliday Connors Cosmopulos, Boston (CD)
Fred Bertino (AD) Wendy Lewis (CW) Baxter
Taylor (P) Matt Mahurin

**Norwegian Breweries (A) JBR, Oslo
(AD) Einar Fuoesne (CW) Kjetil Try**

How many ads show the worst
effects of their product? Norwegian
Breweries allowed the agency to show
unappealing shots of drunks, with the
headlines 'We make a very good
product, but are not always proud of
the result' and 'If this is the only way to
sell more, we don't want to sell more'.

Warning:
In
Minnesota
They Shoot
Drunk
Drivers.

In this state, if you're stopped for drunk driving you can be videotaped, providing
evidence that can be used against you. So don't drink and drive, or you'll be shot on site.

MADD.

**Mothers Against Drunk Driving (A) Clarity
Coverdale Fury, Minneapolis (AD) Rob
Dalton (CW) Jerry Fury (P) Steve Umland**

Let this be a warning.
Not a death threat.

Death

Observer Magazine (AD) Graham Mitchener (P) Nick Georghiou

We all die sometime. The question is when ... and how? And can we do anything to avoid it happening sooner rather than later? The grim reaper was commissioned for a magazine cover to introduce a series of ecological articles on the misuse of land. The image was also used as a poster to promote that issue.

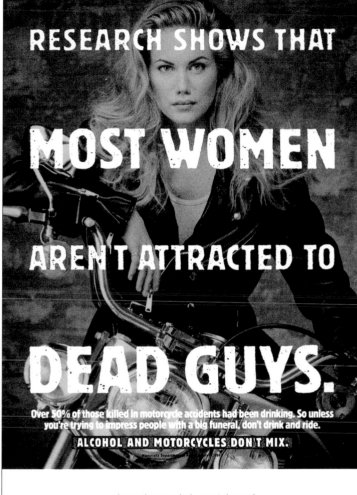

RESEARCH SHOWS THAT MOST WOMEN AREN'T ATTRACTED TO DEAD GUYS.

Over 50% of those killed in motorcycle accidents had been drinking. So unless you're trying to impress people with a big funeral, don't drink and ride.

ALCOHOL AND MOTORCYCLES DON'T MIX.

Ads posted in men's bathrooms in bars and restaurants frequented by bikers.

Minnesota Department of Public Safety (A) Clarity Coverdale Fury, Minneapolis (AD) Jac Coverdale (CW) Josh Denberg (P) Steve Umland

Over 50% of those killed in motorcycle accidents have been drinking. These ads were posted in men's bathrooms in bars and restaurants frequented by bikers.

Only one person has ever risen from the dead. Don't forget that when you're on the roads this Easter.

The human body is a fragile thing. We bruise easily. We cut easily. And we die easily.

But somehow all that is forgotten the moment we get behind the steering wheel of a car.

No-one chooses to die in car accidents. They die through carelessness.

Ask yourself this. When did you last bother to check your tyres for excessive wear? Forgetting to check them can easily result in disaster.

That's why all this week (until 5pm Thursday) we're offering free tyre safety inspections at all Beaurepaires outlets.

Your car will only be off the road for a matter of minutes, cost you nothing and could well save you a lot of trouble later.

It may even save your life.

Beaurepaires
Free tyre safety checks until Easter.

Beaurepaires (A) Colenzo, Wellington, New Zealand (AD) Roger Ginsberg (CW) John O'Leary

This looks like another ad for alcohol-free driving. If you drink and drive, someone's going to get hurt - perhaps terminally. But this is not a public service announcement. Although clothed in altruism, it's actually commercially-driven: 'Let us check to see if you need to buy our product to make you safer.'

SOMETIMES IT TAKES A FAMILY OF FOUR TO STOP A DRUNK DRIVER.

This family of four has already stopped one drunk driver. It is our hope they'll stop thousands more. MADD

Mothers Against Drunk Driving (A) Clarity Coverdale Fury,
Minneapolis (AD) Jac Coverdale (CW) Jerry Fury (P) Steve Umland

If you're not selling anything, and don't even need to be liked,
your advertising can be aggressive to the point of belligerence.
Enhanced by a strong, unshakable conviction that you're in the
right, you can mouth off as vociferously and voraciously as you
like at the brainless murderers.

GUESS WHAT THOUSANDS OF DRUNK DRIVERS AND BUGS HAVE IN COMMON EACH YEAR?

NO BRAINS.

Mothers Against Drunk Driving
(A) Clarity Coverdale Fury, Minneapolis
(AD) Jac Coverdale (CW) Joe Alexander
(P) Steve Umland

Benetton (A) In-house, Italy (AD) Oliviero Toscani (P) Franco Zecchin, Magnum

The aftermath, the bloodbath. The sorrow. The reflection. The ad ran only in Italy.
 Does the use of violent documentary images for advertising strip such tragedies of their dignity? Does painful emotion have a place in advertising, other than gritty health warnings and charity ads?
 Imagine you were selling shirts. After years of pushing playful pastiches of colourfully cosmopolitan kids prancing around, wouldn't you find major global issues more exciting, more energizing, more vital?
 The pictures are not captioned so that they 'have an opportunity to represent greater truths and values,' says Tibor Kalman, head of the communications design firm M&Co and editor-in-chief of the Benetton magazine *Colors*.

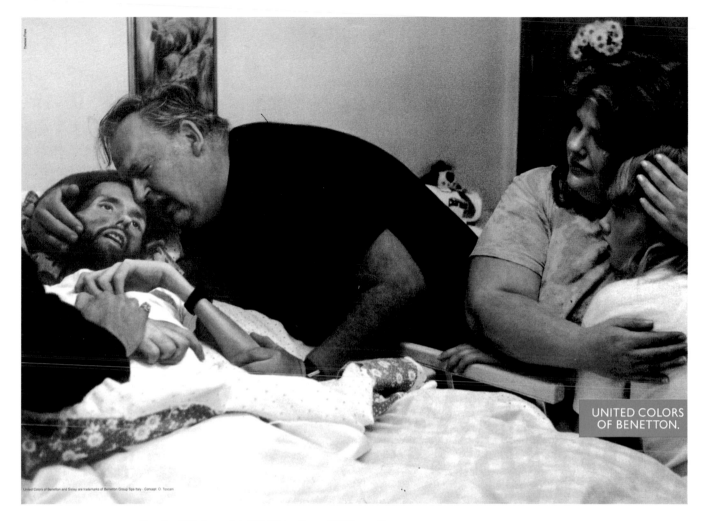

United Colors of Benetton and Sisley are trademarks of Benetton Group Spa Italy · Concept: O. Toscani

UNITED COLORS
OF BENETTON.

Benetton (A) In-house, Italy (AD) Oliviero Toscani (P) Therese Frare

Benetton changed from the symbolic studio images of colourful black and white frivolity to a hornet's nest of controversy. The spring 1992 campaign left the studio and addressed real world issues with real life photographs. David Kirby's deathbed scene and the Mafia murder were originally shot in black and white, then colourized for the campaign. 'We wanted to get away from the artiness of black and white. What the company got into, however, was controversy over colourization' says Tibor Kalman.

  The dying AIDS sufferer, photographed in a hospice in Columbus, Ohio, originally appeared in *Life* in November 1990. The Kirby family believe the picture has the power to create compassion for people with AIDS, and condoned this usage.

Gay serial killer **still** at large.

AIDS. 15,814 HIV positive. 5025 dead. And counting.

INFORMATION AND SUPPORT. 071 735 8171.

Act-Up London (A) WCRS, London (AD & illustrator) Andy Dibb

After initial hesitation, the ad was picked up by the gay, dance and alternative press.

There's only one pullover this photograph should be used to sell.

SILENCE=DEATH. ACT UP.

Information and donations: ACT UP London, BM Box 2995, London WC1 N3X.

Act-Up London (A) WCRS, London (CD) Alan Tilby (AD) Andy Dibb (CW) Gary Knight (P) Dave Stewart

Benetton ads spawned a flurry of spoofs and spinoffs, further fuelled by the public outcry inspired by each successive campaign. The more relevant derivatives successfully reject the host campaign, reposition the ad and restate the message.

ONE OF THESE WOMEN HAS AIDS. NOW WHICH ONE ARE YOU GOING TO PICK UP?

AIDS. IT'S NOT WORTH THE GAMBLE.

AIDS Awareness (A) McCann Erickson, Singapore (CD) Bob Ward

AIDS. Russian roulette. Not worth the gamble.

London Fire Brigade (A) McCann
Erickson, London (AD/CW) Toby
Talbot/Jeneal Rohrback (P) Jim Arnould

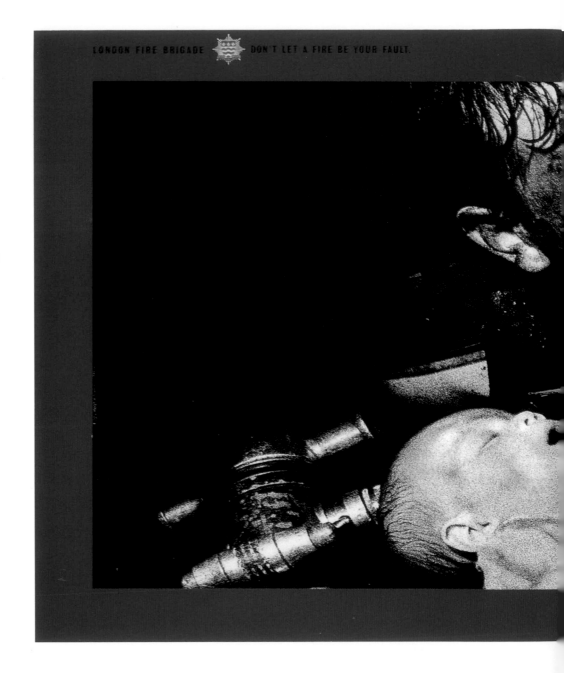

A DEAD BATTERY
IS EASIER TO REPLACE.

MAINTAIN YOUR SMOKE ALARM.

Conscience Stabbers

Trouw (A) DDB, Amsterdam (CD) Lode Schaeffer/Erik Wünsch (AD) Lode Schaeffer (CW) Erik Wünsch (P) Aernout Overbeeke

The heading is a well-known phrase from a well-known dishwasher commercial in Holland: 'Do you still find bits of lasagne after washing up?' The billboard poster draws on a shared experience to evoke shared guilt, using contrast to put our lives in context and in perspective. As a socially responsible newspaper, *Trouw* has its finger on the pulse, because *Trouw* listens.

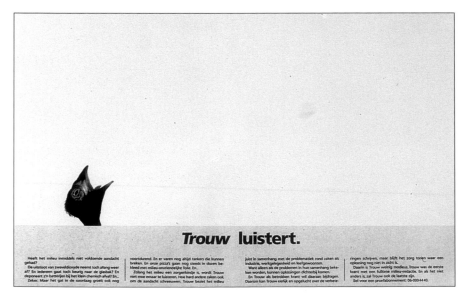

Trouw (A) DDB, Amsterdam (CD) Lode Schaeffer/Erik Wünsch (AD) Lode Schaeffer (CW) Erik Wünsch (P) Hans Kroeskamp (Modelmaker) Scientific Art Studio

Haven't we devoted enough attention to the environment already? After all, sulphur dioxide emissions are dropping. We all take our waste glass to the bottle bank. And we take our used batteries to the chemical waste depot. And ... True enough. But the hole in the ozone layer is growing steadily. And there are still tankers sailing the ocean that can break in two. And our pizzas still come in cartons lined with ecologically unsound foil. And ...

As long as the environment is a source of great concern, *Trouw* will not tire of listening. However insistently other matters clamour for attention. *Trouw* sees the environment as part and parcel of all the other problems involving industry, employment and ways of living. Because only when these problems are considered in the right context will solutions come within reach.

Ever wondered why photographers get there before the aid charities?

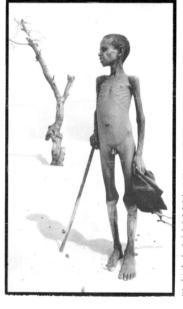

They have no political affiliations.
They move fast.
They travel light.
They do whatever it takes to get results, not discriminating against race, creed or religion.
They don't let bureaucracy get in their way.
They get to the heart of the problem and then bear witness and speak out against atrocities.
By the way, that's Medecins Sans Frontieres we're talking about.
It's why photographers often use our convoys to get to the disasters first.
If you'd like to see 87p of every £1 go directly to the field, complete the coupon.

I enclose a cheque/postal order (payable to Medecins Sans Frontieres UK)
for: £10 £20 £50 £150 Other £
Tick this box if you would like a receipt
I authorise the Charities Aid Foundation, ref. 400205 acting on behalf of M.S.F to debit my Visa/Mastercard/Charity Card/ Diners Club.
Card No.
Today's Date   Card expiry date
Signature
Mr/Mrs/Miss/Ms.   Address
Postcode   Telephone

Life is a human right.

MEDECINS
SANS FRONTIERES

PLEASE SEND THE COUPON AND YOUR DONATION TO: MÉDECINS SANS FRONTIÈRES, PO BOX 158, NORTHAMPTON, NN5 7WB. ENGLISH CHARITY REG. NO. 1026588

Médecins Sans Frontières (A) McCann Erickson, London (AD) John Scully (CW) Jan van Mesdag (P) Sebastiao Salgado

Human rights versus human wrongs. Raise awareness, then raise money. No prevarication. No procrastination. People power can move monoliths. Even dictatorships can be made to yield to public pressure - if it is powerful enough. Over a thousand new supporters were recruited within two weeks of the publication of this campaign.

**Workaid (A) Publicis, London
(AD) Rick Ward (CW) Noel Sharman
(P) Jack Bankhead**

Malnutrition. Oh yes, we know about
that. We have become immune to
the pathetic scenes of human tragedy.
The basic facts seldom encroach on
our conscience.

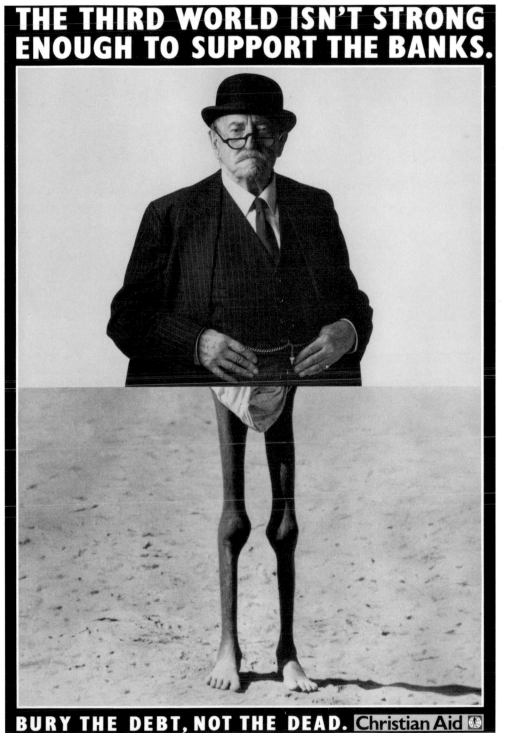

THE THIRD WORLD ISN'T STRONG ENOUGH TO SUPPORT THE BANKS.

BURY THE DEBT, NOT THE DEAD. Christian Aid

Christian Aid (A) Bainsfair Sharkey Trott, London (AD) David Trott

The love of money is the root of all kinds of evil (1 Timothy 6,10)

Environmental Challenge Fund (A) Hill Holliday/Altschiller, New York

The pen is mighty, but vested interests are mightier. Write to those with power and tell them that all our interests lie in their using their power wisely.

Save a Planet, Sacrifice a Congressman.

Congressman _____
US House of Representatives
Washington, D.C. 20515

Dear Congressman,

Your job is on the line. This is not a time for sitting on your duff or someone else will soon be occupying your Congressional seat.

The earth is on a collision course. I would like to know what concrete steps you are proposing to save our planet.

Every day we face unprecedented ecological disasters. There is too much garbage. What can we do about it? There is mass starvation in the world, and massive contamination of our resources right here at home. How can we change that? There are too many people being born, and too many species dying off. We are burning energy recklessly, and breathing in noxious fumes helplessly. How can we begin to reverse this mess?

I'd like you to make the welfare of the earth your top priority. I'd like to know what you're doing, and what I can do on a local level to help.

I want to hear from you. If not, you lose my vote. And you're out.

Your constituent,

**Tear this out, or put your concerns about our planet into your own words.
Either way, let your representatives in Congress know how you feel.**
To further study by students interested in preserving our environment, an Environmental Challenge Fund has been established.
To help, send your donation to: **The Environmental Challenge Fund**, Radio City Station, P.O. Box 1138 New York, NY 10101-1138

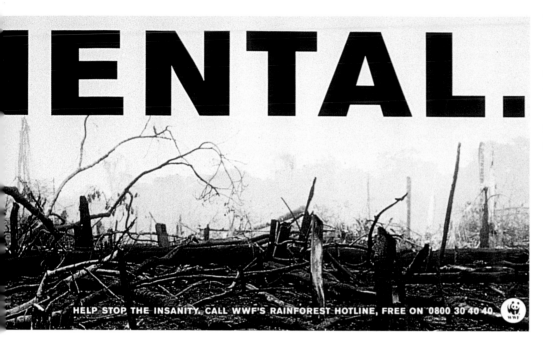

HELP STOP THE INSANITY. CALL WWF'S RAINFOREST HOTLINE, FREE ON 0800 30 40 40.

Worldwide Fund for Nature (A) TBWA, London (AD) Steve Chetham (CW) Trevor Beattie (P) Stockshot

We're custodians of the world. If we mess this one up, we won't get another. Environ Mental was designed specifically to fit twin poster sites with adjacent billboards.

RESEARCHERS SAY THE CURE FOR CANCER MAY BE HIDDEN IN THE RAINFORESTS.

LET'S HOPE IT'S IN HERE.

AND WASN'T IN HERE.

With the Nature Conservancy's Adopt An Acre program, a $35 donation protects one acre of rainforest. In return, we'll send you or someone you name an Honorary Land Deed and periodic conservation Reports From the Field. So save an acre today. Who knows, it could one day save you.

I will adopt _____ acres of rainforest at $35 an acre.

Nature Conservancy (A) Earle Palmer Brown, Maryland (CD) Tom Darbyshire (AD) Paul Safsel (CW) Erhan Erdem (P) Nature Conservancy Stock

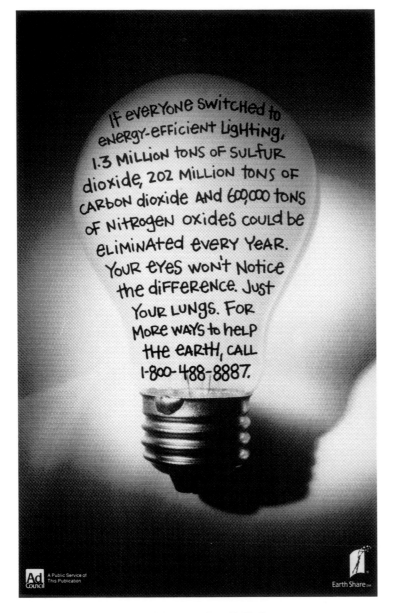

**Earthshare (A) DDB Needham Worldwide,
New York (CDs) Mike Rogers/John Staffen
(AD) John Staffen (CW) Mike Rogers**

**Earthshare (A) DDB Needham Worldwide,
New York (CDs) Mike Rogers/Jack
Mariucci/Bob Mackall (AD) John Staffen
(CW) Mike Rogers**

Earthshare (A) DDB Needham Worldwide, New York (CDs) Mike Rogers/John Staffen (AD) John Staffen (CW) Mike Rogers

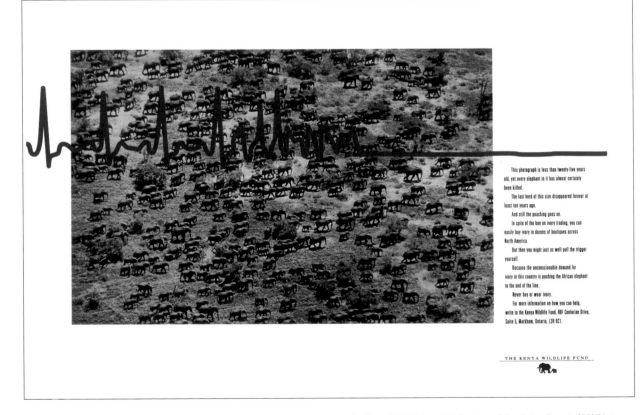

This photograph is less than twenty-five years old, yet every elephant in it has almost certainly been killed.

The last herd of this size disappeared forever at least ten years ago.

And still the poaching goes on.

In spite of the ban on ivory trading, you can easily buy ivory in dozens of boutiques across North America.

But then you might just as well pull the trigger yourself.

Because the unconscionable demand for ivory in this country is pushing the African elephant to the end of the line.

Never buy or wear ivory.

For more information on how you can help, write to the Kenya Wildlife Fund, 00F Centurion Drive, Suite 5, Markham, Ontario, L3R 8C1.

THE KENYA WILDLIFE FUND

The Kenya Wildlife Fund (A) Anderson Advertising, Toronto (CD) Dieter Kaufmann (AD) Dieter Kaufmann (CW) Irene Brenton (P) Peter Beard

Don't be lulled into complacency by reports of increasing elephant populations. The Sisyphian climb has barely begun. And elephants are an exception in the stampede to extinction.

SADLY, HE CAN NEVER FORGET THE PRICE HIS MOTHER PAID FOR THE IVORY YOU BOUGHT.

The Kenya Wildlife Fund (A) Anderson Advertising, Toronto (CD) Dieter Kaufmann (AD) Dieter Kaufmann (CW) Irene Brenton (P) Peter Beard

Returning to the scene of horrific violence, this baby elephant stood dazed beside the mutilated carcass of his dead mother.

His trunk explored the ragged holes where tusks had been cut away by whining chain saws. A once majestic creature butchered to create an ivory accent piece for some foreign coffee table.

Without his mother to care for him, he is unlikely to survive. Without the next generation, the species itself will perish.

Driven to the brink of extinction, the African elephant can regenerate only at a painfully slow pace. Females produce but a single calf every 4 to 5 years. And the older bull elephants they usually mate with have been killed off in record numbers.

Despite the CITES trade ban, a scandalous amount of ivory is still being bought in North America. Clearly, to kill the ivory trade we must kill the demand.

Please, never buy or wear ivory. And give what you can to the Kenya Wildlife Fund.

Your generosity will never be forgotten. For more information on how you can help, contact THE KENYA WILDLIFE FUND, 80 F Centurian Drive, Suite 5, Markham, Ontario, Canada L3R 8C1.

THE KENYA WILDLIFE FUND

It takes up to 40 dumb animals to make a fur coat.

But only one to wear it.

LYNX
Fighting the fur trade

If you don't want animals gassed, electrocuted, trapped or strangled, don't buy a fur coat. P O Box 509 Dunmow, Essex Tel: 0371 2016

Photo: David Bailey

Lynx (A) Yellowhammer, London (AD) Jeremy Pemberton (P) David Bailey

Familiarity softens the blow. If this ad is familiar, look again and let your imagination rest on its implications. See the live animal inside the fur surrendering its body to satisfy someone's desire for status. Greenpeace initiated the ad, but then withdrew it in the face of pressure from fur trapping communities in Canada. The British team running the campaign decided to form a new organization, Lynx, to continue the cause. David Bailey's poster and TV commercial became classics of 'issue advertising'.

If you don't bring your used oil in now, someone will pick it up later.

Used oil poured down drains finds its way to the sea and kills birds and fish. Used oil poured into the ground poisons it. Used oil brought back to a collection point at a selected Mobil station helps. Please bring your used oil back to any Mobil station displaying the Mobil 'Used Oil Collected Here' sign.

Mobil

Environmental Awareness

Mobil Oil (A) Colenzo, Wellington, New Zealand (CD) Daryl Watt (AD) Daryl Watt (CW) Craig Love (P) Daryl Watt

When the Government killed the dog licence they left us to kill the dogs.

One thousand dogs are killed in Britain every day.

For the most part, healthy dogs and puppies with years of life left in them.

The killings take place at local vets, in RSPCA centres and other animal charities throughout the country.

The dogs are given an overdose of anaesthetic and die within seconds.

A van makes regular collections and the dead dogs are taken to the local incinerator.

It doesn't take long to turn a Jock, Spot or Sandy into a small pile of ashes.

This daily slaughter is strange work for a society founded to prevent cruelty to animals.

We hate the killing.

We are sick of doing the Government's dirty work behind closed doors.

We want you to help us force through a dog registration scheme.

The dogs we kill are homeless dogs. Unwanted, or strays left to roam the streets and parks, often in packs.

There are at least 500,000 of them out there right now.

Left to themselves, the figure would be close to 4 million in ten years' time.

Homeless dogs cause road accidents, attack livestock and foul our parks and pavements.

And yet we can't blame the dogs, for we live in a society that makes it more difficult to own a television than a living, breathing creature.

There is no licence required. The Government abolished the licence last year and we are now seeing the consequences.

The RSPCA want to see a dog registration scheme introduced.

And so it seems do most of you. In a recent poll, 92% of you said "yes" to registration.

If there was a registration fee it would encourage responsible dog-ownership.

Each dog could be identified with a number so that its owner could be traced and held responsible for the dog's actions.

The money raised would finance a national dog warden scheme, more efficient clean-up operations and more education for dog-owners.

These measures seem so sensible you wonder why they haven't been tried before.

Well, many of them have.

Sweden, America, Germany, Australia, Russia, France and Ireland all have a more enlightened policy than Britain.

Help us catch up.

Write to your MP and press for dog registration.

If you're not sure how to go about it, call free on 0800 400478 and we'll give you an action-pack and add your name to our petition.

Do it now, for every day that goes by sees another 1,000 dogs put down.

And what kind of society kills healthy dogs?

RSPCA

Registration, not extermination.

Royal Society for the Prevention of Cruelty to Animals (RSPCA) (A) Abbott Mead Vickers/BBDO, London (AD) Ron Brown (CW) David Abbott (P) Derek Seagrim

Shock breaks through our apathy and evokes our sympathy. But how intrusive can an ad be before it begins to be counterproductive and alienate even the target market?

National Canine Defence League (A) TBWA, London
(AD) Steve Chetham (CW) Trevor Beattie (P) Leon (M) Trotsky

DEAR SANTA.

DON'T EVEN THINK ABOUT IT.

A DOG IS FOR LIFE, NOT JUST FOR CHRISTMAS.

NATIONAL CANINE DEFENCE LEAGUE

**National Canine Defence League (A) TBWA, London
(AD) Steve Chetham (CW) Trevor Beattie (P) Leon**

Words Make The Picture

Billy Graham (A) Chiat Day, Toronto
(AD) Duncan Bruce (CW) Aubrey Singer

'Love keeps no record of wrongs.'
(1 Corinthians 13, 5)

AdultClassified   461-7889

Jesus will love you for free.

Unconditionally. No matter who you are. No matter where you're coming from. Come hear Billy Graham's message of love and hope. Even the admission's free.

BILLY GRAHAM & FRIENDS
JUNE 7-11, SKYDOME

Levi Strauss & Co (A) Bartle Bogle Hegarty, London (CD) John Hegarty (AD) Rosie Arnold (CW) Charles Hendley (P) Mary Ellen Mark

The image is the antithesis of the target market. Yet jeans wearers are cool enough to use unhip people - as long as it's to laugh at them. If you're old, you're out of it. It's hard to be hip, but is it hip to be hard?

They're what the gardener wears aren't they?

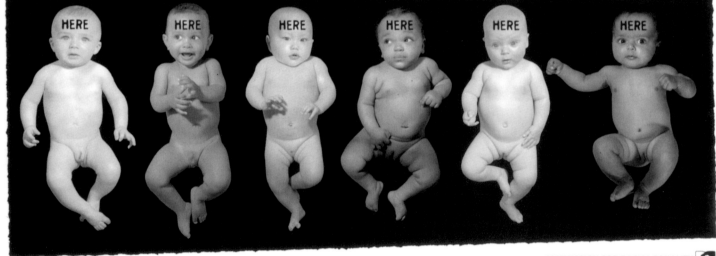

**Commission for Racial Equality (A) Saatchi and Saatchi, London
(AD) Ajab Samrai Singh (CW) Giles Montgomery (P) Alastair Thain**

There are some 120,000 incidents a year of racial harassment,
abuse, assault, arson and murder. This high profile campaign
began with the point that racist behaviour is not natural in any
way. None of us are born racists - it is learnt behaviour.

"I'm Not Prejudiced. I Just Don't Like Him."

THERE'S NO EXCUSE FOR PREJUDICE.

**Anti-Defamation League of B'nai B'rith
(A) Earle Palmer Brown, Maryland**

They are not even euphemisms. They're lies. How often do we fail to be truthful to ourselves, let alone others?

While few people have ever been hit over the head with a frying pan, many have been hit in the heart. The prostate gland. And the colon.

Because fried foods, as part of a high-fat diet, may increase the risk of heart disease as well as certain kinds of cancer — including breast cancer.

Fortunately, you can reduce the fat in your diet by substituting baked, broiled and boiled foods when possible. And by using a non-stick pan when you do fry, with little or no fat.

For a free booklet on low-fat eating, call 1-800-EAT-LEAN.

After all, the purpose of food is to sustain life, not take it away.

1-800-EAT-LEAN

LAST YEAR 400,000 WOMEN KILLED THEIR HUSBANDS WITH A FRYING PAN.

A public service message from The Henry J. Kaiser Family Foundation.

(A) Levine Huntley Vick & Beaver, New York
(AD) Richard Ostroff (P) Cailor Resnick

You can't get more mundane than this picture: it's the words that hit you.

THE MOST EXPENSIVE GOWNS AREN'T FROM CALVIN KLEIN, BILL BLASS, OR YVES ST. LAURENT.

Do you believe this?

Last year, the average cost of a designer gown was about $3,000. But the average cost of a hospital gown and stay was about $4,800.*

And you thought high fashion was expensive.

Hospitals and doctors aren't solely responsible for driving health care costs up. Utilization, new technology and catastrophic claims all contribute to the rising cost of employee health benefits. Which, incidentally, are expected to increase this year an average of 16.5%.**

Is there any way to control these ever-rising costs?

At NWNL Group, our experience shows us the answer is yes. But the solution is not to give you a low rate just to get your business, and a big increase a year later to make up for it. Instead, we ask you to make some tough but fair choices about your benefits program.

We'll help you identify what those choices are and we'll show you how they could affect your plan. For example, our catastrophic case management program could save you thousands of dollars.

Our special booklet – *Case Management: What Works, What Doesn't* – will tell you more about this approach to cost control. For a copy, call or write Rick Naymark, NWNL Group, Box 20, Minneapolis, MN 55440. (612) 342-7137.

Considering what your costs are, you can't afford gaps in your coverage.

NORTHWESTERN NATIONAL LIFE INSURANCE COMPANY

**Northwestern National Life
(A) Clarity Coverdale Fury, Minneapolis
(AD) Jac Coverdale (CW) Jerry Fury
(P) Shawn Michienzi**

It's easier to spend money on visible trinkets that bring immediate and obvious gratification. More difficult to persuade someone of the benefits of spending money for delayed gratification, with the possibility of no pay-off at all.

**Reckitt & Colman/Dettol (A) Naga DDB
Needham, Malaysia (CD) Alan Lim
(AD) Sarah Goh/Jo Ho (CW) Sean Sim
(P) Pashe Studio**

Ummm. Enough to turn you into a bleach freak.

There's a lot of advertising for things nobody wants - heart disease, AIDS, cancer, infection...

If you think this is disgusting, wait till you taste their vomit.

Unfortunately, flies breed pretty fast in tropical climates. In a few days, their young will be fully-grown and frequenting the dirtiest places you can imagine. And they have this nasty habit of regurgitating stuff from their gut as they feed. Onto your food. It's no surprise then that diseases spread so easily. Cover all foodstuff and use a little antiseptic liquid to keep your hands and kitchen area clean. For the sake of your health, and appetite. †**Dettol** protects in many ways.

Art Center College of Design
Library
1700 Lida Street
Pasadena, Calif. 91103

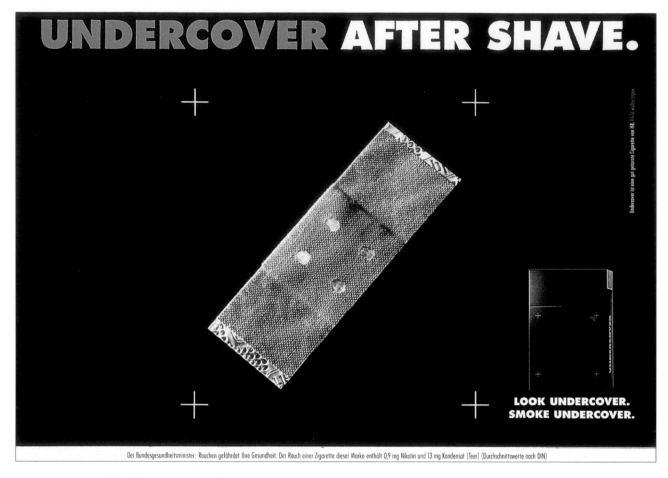

**BAT Undercover Cigarettes (A) Grey, Düsseldorf (CD) Thomas Heuter
(AD) Jochen Heimann (CW) Werner Busam (P) Archim Straub**

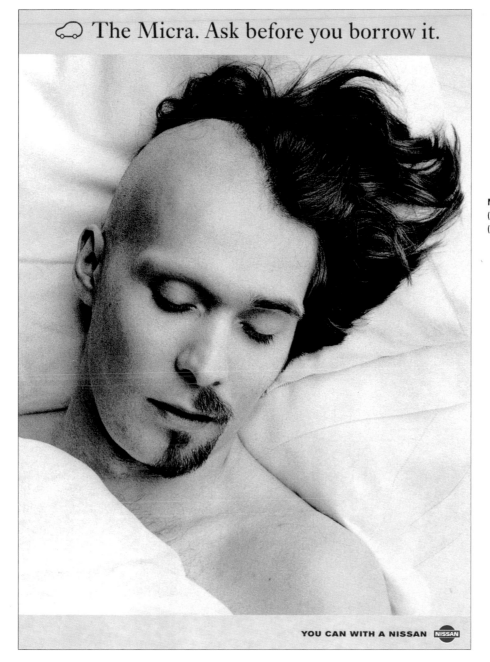

Nissan Micra (A) TBWA, London
(AD) Chris Hodgkiss (CW) Pip Bishop
(P) John Claridge

Jarring Juxtapositions

Royal British Legion (A) Delaney Fletcher Bozell, London (AD) Steve Donoghue (CW) John Peake (P) Stock

Imagine a hammer and sickle in the raised hand of the statue in New York Harbour. What a liberty! Or the Star of David flying over Mecca. Or McDonalds in Tokyo or Moscow ... What? The commercial invasion of the world is already in full swing? Is nothing sacred?

GIVE THANKS.

IN 1939, THIS WAS MORE THAN JUST ONE MAN'S DREAM.

IT WAS CLOSE TO BECOMING A REALITY.

ONLY OUR ARMED FORCES STOOD BETWEEN US AND OBLIVION.

THEY GAVE THEIR ALL TO STOP THE SEEMINGLY UNSTOPPABLE.

HUNDREDS OF THOUSANDS GAVE THEIR LIVES.

THE POPPY IS THEIR SYMBOL.

LAST YEAR, BETWEEN US WE GAVE AN AVERAGE OF 20p FOR EVERY POPPY WE BOUGHT.

20p A POPPY FOR THE 8 MILLION EX-SERVICEMEN AND WOMEN STILL CARED FOR BY THE ROYAL BRITISH LEGION.

20p A POPPY FOR THEIR 10 MILLION DEPENDANTS.

20p A POPPY FOR THE FREEDOMS WE ENJOY TODAY.

20p.

GIVE A DAMN. **GIVE A POUND.**

Kadu Clothing (A) Ben-ja-min(d), London (ADs) Adam Hunt/Ben Nott (CWs) Ben Nott/Adam Hunt (P) Diederik Kratz

Shock with a purpose: the surfwear is tough. And hyperbole is one of advertising's most powerful tools. So this is more relevant, more justifiable than much of Benetton's advertising, to which this campaign has been compared. Yet, Kadu sales soared as a result, whereas the public boycotted Benetton. Also, the ads appeared in surfers' magazines, not emblazoned across billboards.

Two fatal shark attacks occurred in Australia at the same time the disembowelled shark ad appeared. This caused media outrage and applause. The cockroach ad appeared a few days after the anniversary of the bombing of Hiroshima. Totally ridiculous situations often prompt total recall.

Kadu Clothing (A) Andromeda, Sydney (AD) Paul Bennell/Ben Nott (CW) Ben Nott/Paul Bennell (P) Simon Harsent (Stylist) Adam Hunt

Gallaher/Silk Cut (A) M&C Saatchi, London (AD) Carlos (CW) Keith Bickel (P) Masatomo Kuriya

The Silk Cut campaign was born in 1983 when Paul Arden and Charles Saatchi grappled with the problem facing all cigarette advertising. In fact, the stringent restrictions - designed to protect the public - ended up treating them to a kaleidoscope of inventive images. For the fly-catcher clenching the wrong fly, the photographer was chosen because of his set of beautiful sunflower photographs that were on show at the Van Gogh Museum.

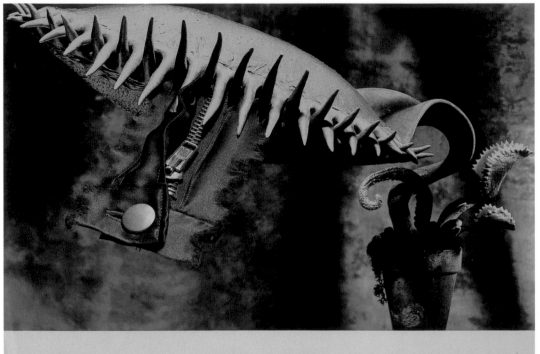

7mg TAR 0·7mg NICOTINE
SMOKING CAUSES HEART DISEASE
Health Departments' Chief Medical Officers

SMOKING CAUSES FATAL DISEASES
Chief Medical Officers' Warning
5mg Tar   0.5mg Nicotine

Gallaher/Silk Cut (A) M&C Saatchi, London (AD) Martha Reilly (CW) Richard Dean (P) Nadav Kander (Modelmakers) Matthew Wurr & Co

Despite efforts to have cigarette advertising snuffed out, the creative embers are endlessly rekindled to draw consumers' attention. Cigarettes may kill you, but cigarette advertising can set your imagination alight with some of the most innovative and intriguing advertising of the last three decades. Given the simple concept of purple silk and a cut, how many variations can you create?

**Gallaher/Silk Cut (A) Saatchi & Saatchi, London (AD) Peter Gibb
(CW) James Lowther (P) Sebastiao Salgado**

In a perhaps cynical echo of his Brazilian gold mine workers,
Magnum photographer Sebastiao Salgado was asked to execute
a Silk Cut ad featuring the mudmen of Papua New Guinea.

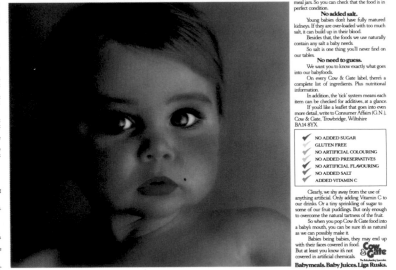

Cow & Gate (A) Abbott Mead Vickers/BBDO, London (AD) Andy Arghyrou
(CW) Lynda Richardson (P) Steve Cavalier

Man as art shocks when presented out of context. Ladies' make-up on a baby, however tastefully applied, pierces our sensibilities more deeply than self-imposed tattoos or safety pins.

**British Gas (A) Young & Rubicam, London (AD) Trevor Melvin (CW)
Jeanne Willis (P) Michael Portelly (M) Lauren Heston/Billy Zeqiri**

The idea for a television commercial, which also appeared on
the billboards, came from a magazine article about Russian
babies swimming underwater. During screen tests with the
babies, it was found that they were doing things naturally
that were written on the storyboard. There was no question
of coercion. Four babies were taken to the Red Sea. Each one
could be in the water for only three or four minutes at a time,
and underwater for up to 10 seconds at a time.

Kodak (A) J. Walter Thompson, Milan
(CD) Dario Diaz (AD) Luca Maroni
(CW) Enrico Chiarugi (P) Jack Casale

Benetton (A) In-house, Italy
(AD) Oliviero Toscani

Benetton (A) In-house, Italy (AD) Oliviero Toscani

NEW
WIDE
BODY
TWIN
CAMRY.

TOYOTA

Toyota Motor Corporation Australia (A) Saatchi & Saatchi,
Sydney (CD) Bob Isherwood (AD) Peter Kirwan (CW) Michael
Syme (P) Stuart Crossett

Toyota Motor Corporation Australia
(A) Saatchi & Saatchi, Sydney
(CD) Bob Isherwood (AD) Jonathan Teo
(CW) Michael Newman
(P) Michael Skelton

Pon's Automobielhandel B.V. (A) DDB,
Amsterdam (CD) Lode Schaeffer/Erik
Wünsch (AD) Lode Schaeffer (CW) Erik
Wünsch (P) Hans Kroeskamp (Illustrator)
Gottfried Helnwein

Remember those great little VW ads?
None of that self-deprecating modesty
with this Golf VR6. Its 2.8 litre, six
cylinder engine, (128 kw/174 hp), max
speed 112.5km per half hour. Who's
being funny here?

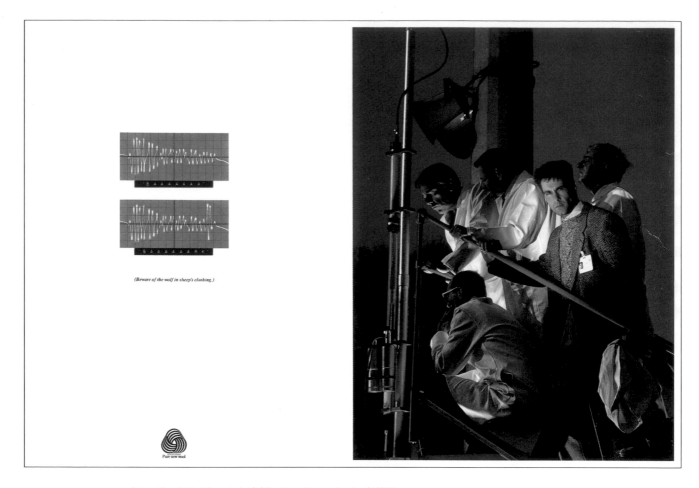

(Beware of the wolf in sheep's clothing.)

International Wool Secretariat (A) Davidson Pearce, London (AD) Kit Marr (CW) Neil Fazakerley (P) Brian Griffin

Soft wool and steely confrontation create tension on the right hand page. You find this uncomfortable, even threatening, and look for a let out. The job of the clever little graphic on the left is to diffuse the tension and draw you in to the word game. The two voice prints look technical, and reflect the technical white coats in the photograph.

**TDK (A) GGK, Milan (AD) Jamie Ambler
(P) Terence Donovan**

A child could do it.

**White Horse Whisky (A) Kingsley
Manton Palmer, London (AD) Mike Kidd
(P) Michael Joseph**

By associating a particular animal with
your product, people will remember it
more readily. This link can be Pavlovian
in its directness. Two terriers mean
whisky, labrador puppies mean toilet
tissue and an old English sheepdog
has now assumed the name of a paint.
A koala can be moaning about only one
airline. A cockerel is not sure whether
it's a breakfast cereal or trendy
sportwear. And as for the white horse ...
Michael Joseph has shot 23 white
horses over the years, and has taken
them just about everywhere.

When you've got a body capable of performing at the highest level, why handicap it?

Nikon lenses, branded Nikkor, represent over seventy years of design expertise and innovation.

Add one to your Nikon body, and you're holding the finest photographic combination in the world. (Perhaps that's why most of the world's top professional photographers use them.)

You'll know how good a Nikkor lens is the moment you pick one up. Individual elements and assemblies are tested and inspected relentlessly to ensure a faultless performance no matter what the circumstances.

Even so, our designers are always searching for ways to improve our existing range of lenses. And, when the need arises, to create new ones.

To enhance light transmission and to give a brighter image in long telephoto lenses, we developed Extra-low Dispersion (ED) glass. (We make over 250 types of our own optical glass.)

And with Nikon Integrated Coating (NIC) we have dramatically increased image contrast and achieved uniform colour balance across the entire range of Nikkor lenses.

Every current Nikkor lens will fit every Nikon body made since the introduction of our famous F-mount in 1959. It's part of what we call 'The System'. An unparalleled range of every conceivable photographic accessory from filters to speedlights.

And now's your chance to start building your own Nikon System.

HOW GOOD IS A NIKON BODY WITHOUT A NIKON LENS?

SAVE UP TO £250 ON NIKON LENSES AND ACCESSORIES WHEN YOU BUY A NIKON BODY AND LENS.

Buy a combination of Nikon body and Nikkor lens between June 1st and August 31st and, on proof of purchase, we'll send you a book of vouchers redeemable against specific Nikon lenses and accessories up to a total value of £250. For details, pick up a leaflet from your local Nikon authorised dealer.

Treat your body well and it will treat you to some of the best pictures you've ever taken.

Nikon

WE TAKE THE WORLD'S GREATEST PICTURES.

For further information, write to Nikon UK Ltd., Nikon House, 380 Richmond Road, Kingston-upon-Thames, Surrey KT2 5PR or telephone 081 541 4440 and ask for extension 'SLR'.

Nikon (A) Delaney Fletcher Bozell, London (AD) Steve Donoghue (CW) John Peake (P) Anthony Crickmay (Inset photo) David Parfitt

Take a principle. Pick a bizarre example. Then illustrate it literally... When you've got a body capable of performing at the highest level, why handicap it?

Perception.

Reality.

If your idea of a Rolling Stone reader looks like a holdout from the 60's, welcome to the 80's. Rolling Stone ranks number one in reaching concentrations of 18-34 readers with household incomes exceeding $25,000. When you buy Rolling Stone, you buy an audience that sets the trends and shapes the buying patterns for the most affluent consumers in America. That's the kind of reality you can take to the bank.

Rolling Stone (A) Fallon McElligott, Minneapolis

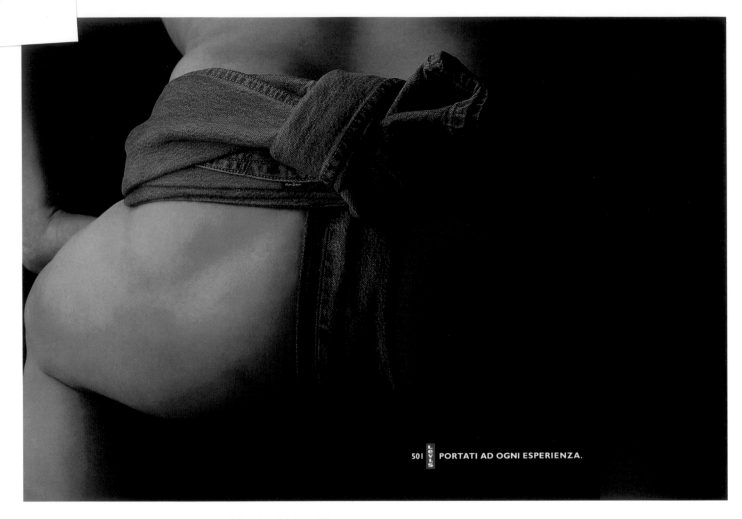

Levi Strauss, (A) McCann Erickson, Milan
(AD) Stefano Colombo (CW) Alessandro
Canale (P) Graham Ford

**DSR Posters (A) Jung/von Matt, Hamburg
(AD) Claudia Wriedt (CW) Mathias Bahn
(P) Uwe Düttmann**

Logic and creativity are uncomfortable
bedfellows. German print advertising
tends to be rational and factual, rather
than arresting and entertaining. But in
a shift from the prosaic to the poetic,
the photographer's brief was to make
the pictures modern, stylish and funny,
and support the headline: Everyone
notices posters - unless they have a
bag over their head.

Alexon (A) Saatchi & Saatchi, London (AD) Paul Arden (P) Richard Avedon

Standing out from the catalogue of clothes ads calls for inventive
thinking - strip the model, bunch the clothes on her head or stretch
them around unlikely parts of the body.

Gentle Jars

Financial Times (A) Delaney Fletcher Bozell, London (AD) Rob Kitchen (CW) Patrick Woodward (P) Jack Bankhead

No FT, no comment.

Get the point?

**De'Longhi (A) ALMAP/BBDO, Sao Paulo
(AD) Marcello Serpa/Simone Drago
(CW) Cassio Zanatta (P) Archive/Alexandre
Catan/ Manolo Moran**

The brief: with a limited budget, make this Italian household brand famous in Brazil. The campaign blends appropriate products with paintings by Caravaggio, Raphael and Tintoretto. By association, the products benefit from the perceived value of the work of art. Another in the series shows Dante's Inferno furnished with an air conditioner. The company's twelve month sales target was achieved within two months.

**Wella Pacific Beauty Care
(A) The Ball Partnership, Singapore
(CD) Robert Speechley
(AD/CW) Neil French (P) Willie Tang**

Unable to specify any hair-restoring claims, the ad implies that the product will grow hair on anything.

**Tesco Stores (A) Lowe Howard-Spink, London (AD) Alan Davis
(CW) Jez Willy (P) Elliott Erwitt**

Sit outside a cafe with Magnum photographer Elliott Erwitt,
and, although he's attentive to the conversation, his eyes
are everywhere and his hand is poised near his Leica.
He's looking for that moment, à la Cartier-Bresson - but with
the added eye for humour.

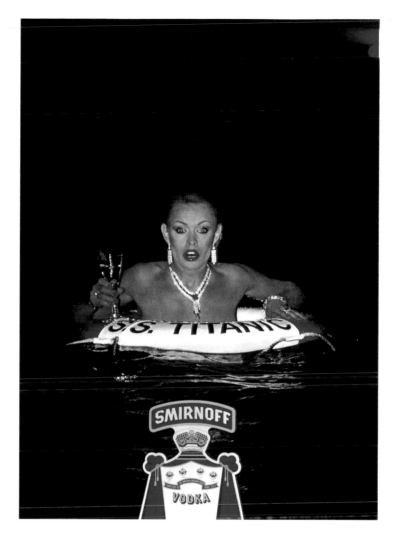

Smirnoff (A) Young & Rubicam, London (AD) Tony Wheeton (P) John Thornton

Well, they said anything could happen. The bejewelled lady appears to be adrift in the middle of the Atlantic, yet she's squatting in two feet of water, very close to the shore.

The early Smirnoff campaign focused on good-humoured - usually ridiculous - illusions: a model water skiing behind a turbo-charged Loch Ness Monster, a team of huskies emerging from a fridge and a German U-boat surfacing in a Hollywood swimming pool. Does it all verge too closely on hallucinations, pink elephants? Drink advertising is almost as touchy a subject as cigarette advertising.

Smirnoff (A) Young & Rubicam, London (AD) Mike Owen (CW) Andy Archer (P) Alan David-Tu

**Smirnoff (A) Lowe Howard-Spink, London
(CD) Paul Weinberger (AD) Brian Campbell
(CW) Paul Falla (P) Mike Parsons**

The Smirnoff campaign went through
several transformations as well as a
change of ad agency, until they reached
the other side, where reality still takes
second place to imagination, and
nothing is quite what it seems. Since
1992, the 'through the bottle' campaign
has run in 59 countries. It targets
sophisticated 18-24 year old drinkers,
who wouldn't identify with anything less
than stylish, mind-expanding advertising.

**NEC (A) Hampel Stefanides, New York
(AD) Dean Stefanides (CW) Larry Hampel
(P) Kenji Toma/Agent Michael Ash**

In yer face. Bigger and brighter,
NEC claim to be creating a whole
new connection between you and
your computer.

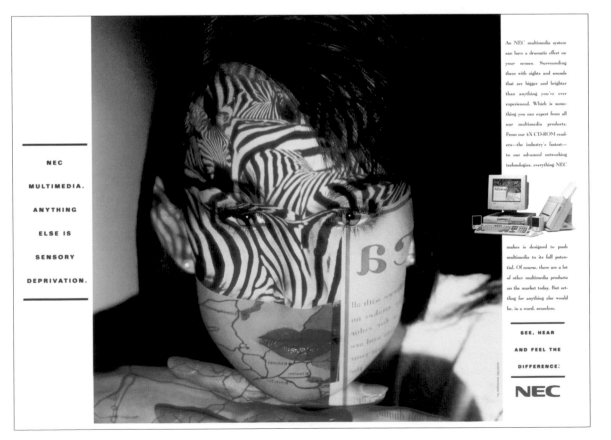

Vrij Uit (A) Benjamens van Doorn Euro RSCG, Amstelveen (AD) Cor den Boer (CW) Aad Kuyyper (P) Miriam Jeurissen

In yer teeth and up yer nose. A larger-than-life image that flies in the face of comfortable ads usually used for such family subjects as motoring holidays.

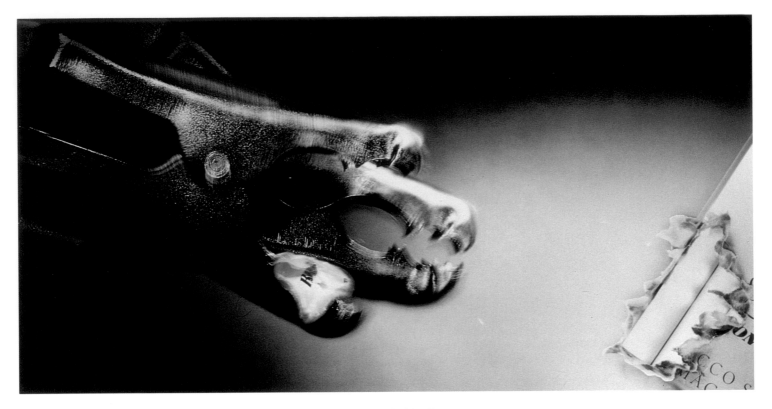

Gallaher, (A) Collett Dickenson Pearce, London (AD) Guy Moore (CW) Tony Malcolm (P) Nick Georghiou

In 1977, Benson & Hedges started all the surreal fun and games when Alan Waldie eschewed all the clichés and took an oblique look at cigarette advertising. His early work - Mouse hole, Bird cage, Stonehenge and Ducks - primed people to expect more subtle visual ideas. You don't have to smoke - just enjoy the ever-changing art gallery. It is a game of intrigue for the artist and the audience to enjoy, without getting their fingers burned or damaging their health. This series of B&H ads featured products from their Gratis catalogue. In this case, jump leads were animated into the head of an alien creature attacking the pack.

**Dunlop (A) Saatchi & Saatchi, London (AD) Roy Askew (CW) David Bourne
(P) John Thornton**

A simple concept, transformed into a literal visual, provides one of
advertising's most powerful tools. The Siamese motorbike was put
together from three separate 5 x 4 transparencies to show that Dunlop
design very different tyres for the front and the back. How do you
know it's not a mirror image? This was retouched manually, in the
days before widespread computer image manipulation.

Dunlop K181s. Because you don't have two front wheels.

Some tyre manufacturers obviously think that your back wheel is the same as your front wheel. And they expect you to whack the same tyres on both wheels.

But Dunlop K181s are specifically designed for each wheel: a ribbed front tyre and a block pattern rear.

And they'll outgrip and outperform anything else on the tarmac. Which is good news for those of us who aren't all that kinky for gravel rash.

A legend in its own lifetime.

In the days when only bikers wore black leather jackets, when the North Circular throbbed with British Iron and a mug of tea at the Ace Caff cost 6d, everyone rode on Dunlop TT100s.

Times change and so did TT100s. Dunlop refined and improved them, and finally rechristened them as K181s, putting more rubber on the road to cope with the increased bhp of the latest bikes, giving you more stability and steering control.

K181s are H-rated for just about every road bike from 250cc to 750cc. The really big boys can get K181 "Qualifiers", V-rated for 750cc's and over with 16"/17"/18" rear wheels.

Living your fantasies.

Some of us are Barry Sheenes, some of us are mean-eyed outlaws on the Pacific Coast Highway, cissy bars glinting in the Californian sun.

But we'd all quite like to stay alive. At least until we're too old to throw a leg across the saddle. With Dunlop K181s you stand a better chance. **DUNLOP**

Wilson and Sons (A) Faulds Advertising, Edinburgh (CD) Simon Scott/Andrew Lindsay (AD) Iain Allan (CW) Adrian Jeffery (P) Richard Mountney

An unexpected relief, that brings an affectionate smile to the lips, is a welcome antidote to all the cruelty highlighted in chapter 6. What more could a manufacturer ask of its advertising?

Jim Beam Windsor Canadian (A) Fallon McElligott, Minneapolis (AD) Tom Lichtenheld (CW) John Stingley (P) Craig Perman (Product shot) Dave Jordano

The campaign comprises a series of (mostly) stock images that fit the strategy. In the face of such frustration, fortunately there's a payoff.

Gillette/Right Guard (A) N.W. Ayer & Partners, New York

Out of context, Hulk Hogan presents a jarring, almost unpalatable picture. The product draws him into the frame with an appropriate word play.

Vaseline (A) Barker McCormac, Johannesburg (CD) Alex McCormac

A line-up of the target market. Lots of babies' bottoms use it, so why not show off the customer base?

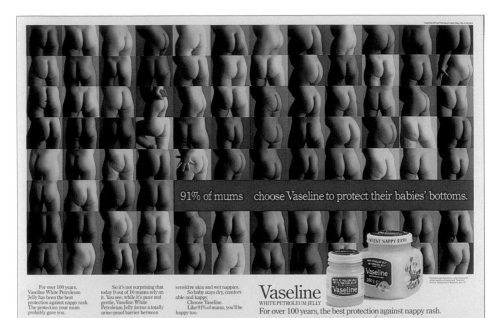

Agency promotion (A) Young & Rubicam, Lisbon

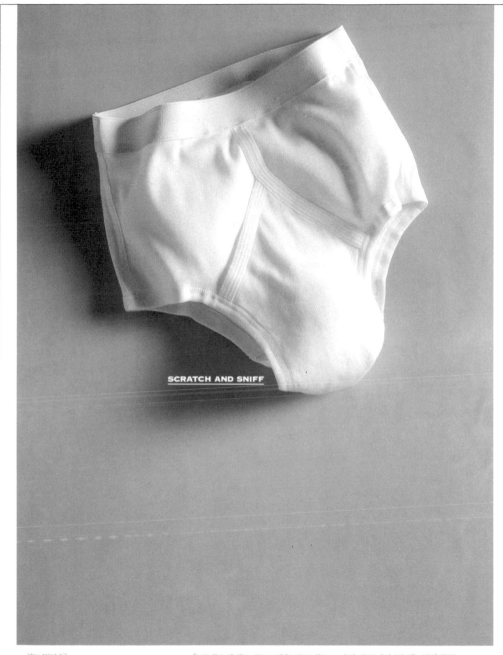

SCRATCH AND SNIFF

Spin (A) Leifitz Jussa Bollasch Erris, Singapore (AD) Neil French (CW) Neil French (P) Hanchew

You tried it?

Seriously? You actually tried it? Phew! Well, full marks for bravery, anyway, if not for intelligence. So, did you smell anything?

Just newspaper, right?

Not as revolting as it might have been, but still, not what you might call a sensual experience.

It's much the same with your clothes.

Even though they may well be clean, they don't really smell clean.

That's why SPIN, the newly-formulated machine-friendly washing-powder, has an added freshening ingredient, that leaves your clothes with just a hint of mountain-fresh fragrance.

So your clothes not only are clean, not only

look clean, but actually smell clean.

Now, you may say you're far too busy to worry about washing powders; that it's none of your business.

But what have you got to lose? Ask your maid to switch to SPIN, and you may be surprised how much business improves.

And that's not to be sniffed at, is it?

Painless Mutilations

We've travelled all over the world for ideas for Habitat's new tribal collection. Drop by if you haven't got too much on your plate.

Habitat (A) Saatchi & Saatchi, London
(AD) Anthony Easton (CW) Adam Kean
(P) Andrew MacPherson

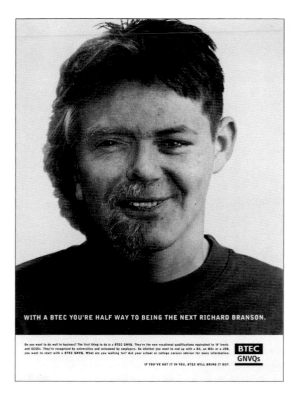

BTEC (A) Publicis, London (AD) Rick Ward
(CW) Noel Sharman (P) Philip Meech

Fusion (A) Simons Palmer Denton Clemmow
& Johnson (D) Andy McKay (P) Brian Griffin

An aura of intensity eminates from much
of Griffin's work. There's often humour,
but it is invariably underscored by a
depth of feeling.

Self-promotion, Brazil (P) Milton Montenegro

Jonathan Sceats Sunglasses (A) Omon,
Sydney (AD) Bobbi Gassy (CW) Siimon
Reynolds (P) John Adams

Soften The Blow

COTTON WOOL

OR BUY A VOLVO.

Volvo (A) Abbott Mead Vickers BBDO, London (AD) Ron Brown (CW) David Abbott (P) Bob Miller

Some of the best car advertising doesn't include the car. With an open brief to produce a poster, the creatives focused on the attribute of safety, and came up with the idea that protection is like being wrapped in cotton wool. No need for the car. The cotton wool is the car. And it's real, shot on a single photograph: two 18 inch rolls wrapped around a wooden drum, which contained a platform for the boy to lie on.

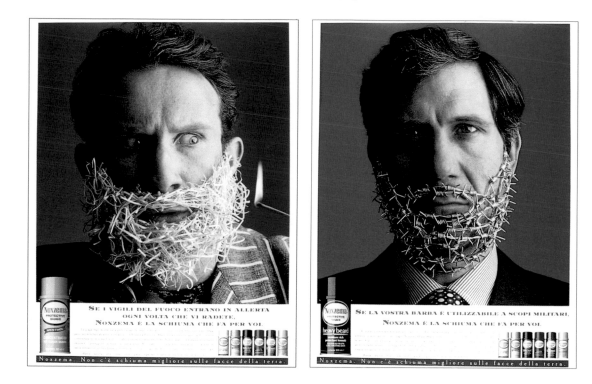

Noxzema (A) McCann Erickson, Milan (CD) Milka Pogliani (AD) Elia Coro (CW) Paolo Chiarabrando (P) Graham Ford

Enough shock to be arresting. Enough wit to be endearing.

Lever Brothers/Comfort (A) Oglivy & Mather, London (AD/CW) Nick Parton/John Bayley (P) Peter Rauter

The TV commercial for the fabric conditioner had exaggerated sound effects accompanying people putting on and taking off clothes. The press ads had to put across the same abrasive message to illustrate the results of not using the product.

In Yer Face

Britvic Soft Drinks (A) Howell Henry Chaldecott Lury & Partners, London (AD) Trevor Robinson (CW) Alan Young (P) Dave McKean

Cuddly? The OTT belligerence of the ad makes it amusing, and therefore comfortable. The no-holds-barred strategies adopted for Tango's campaigns have moved the drink from the dusty back shelf to the third best selling drink in the UK.

Aaron Speiser Acting Workshop (A) The Miller Group, Los Angeles (CD) Renee Miller (AD) Jason Stinsmuehlen (CW) Scott Habetz (P) Jason Stinsmuehlen

Get real ... we are. The shock of the true. Unless we want only safe advertising, we must accept risks. If you're not breaking new ground, you're following.

WEA Records (A) Felipe Taborda Design, Rio de Janeiro (AD) Felipe Taborda (P) Rodrigo Lopes

Rock music feeds on bad taste. Its street cred is enhanced by savage or surreal images which fly in the face of sugar and spice and all things nice. This poster heralded the release of a new album, Carne Crua (Raw Meat) by Barao Vermelho (Red Baron). One man's meat is another man's poisson.

Microplay Video Games (A) Freelance, Toronto (AD) Frank Lepre (CW) Ron MacDonald (P) Chris Gordaneer

A sick joke? Some advertising is more 'Out yer mouth' than 'In yer face'. This video game store invites you to visit for all the latest gut-wrenching, cerebrum-twisting, heart-in-your-throat action. Preferably before lunch.

At Microplay Video Games we buy, rent, trade, sell and repair all video games and systems. So for all the latest gut-wrenching, cerebrum-twisting, heart-in-your-throat action, give us a visit. Preferably before lunch.

Stores nationwide. For location nearest you see listing opposite.

MICROPLAY VIDEO GAMES

We interrupt your regular programming.

Olympus cameras (A) Lowe Howard-Spink, London (AD) Brian Campbell (CW) Ben Priest

Bad taste flaunted like a badge of courage? No, this is tongue-in-cheek humour. Yet there will always be some who take hyperbole at face value.

Harley Davidson produced a series of socially irresponsible ads advocating the neglect of people in favour of buying a motorbike. The tone of voice used sets out to break the boundaries of good taste; 'We don't live in a pretty world', they say, 'and we're talking the language of the target market.'

  And yet ... and yet, their conviction isn't strong enough to allow one of their deliberately shocking ads to appear in a book about shock.

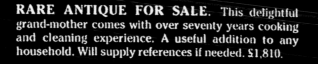

RARE ANTIQUE FOR SALE. This delightful grand-mother comes with over seventy years cooking and cleaning experience. A useful addition to any household. Will supply references if needed. £1,810.

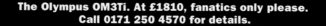

**The Olympus OM3Ti. At £1810, fanatics only please.
Call 0171 250 4570 for details.**

**Linn Hi Fi (A) Marr Associates, Edinburgh (CD) Colin Marr (AD)
Ronnie Malden (CW) Ronnie Malden (P) Paddy Eckersley**

It's not praising the product's attributes, not rubbishing its
rivals. It says you'll rate people who rate Linn Hi-Fi. And you
won't those who don't.

Trouw luistert.

Stel, je hebt als krant de pretentie je betrokken te voelen bij wat de samenleving bezighoudt.
Dan moet je niet alleen berichten over, maar ook de spreekbuis zijn van die samenleving.
En als je daarbij de pretentie hebt open te staan voor alle meningen, dan moet je niet willen uitmaken op welke manier een mening wordt uitgedragen.
Trouw heeft die pretentie.
Trouw geeft alle aandacht aan de zaken die ons allemaal beroeren. Zaken als recessie, werkloosheid en verpaupering.
En Trouw geeft ruimte aan iedereen die daarbij partij is.
Dus hoort u in Trouw niet alleen weloverwogen woorden, maar soms ook een taal die niet de uwe is.
Zonder censuur. Omdat wij geloven dat u zelf uw standpunt kunt bepalen.
Maar niet zonder commentaar. Omdat wij ook een mening hebben.
Waarin we overigens verrassend vaak de kant kiezen van die minder zorgvuldig geformuleerde mening.
Er is geen taal die niet thuishoort in een betrokken krant als Trouw. Dat willen we maar gezegd hebben.
Bel voor een proefabonnement: 06-0994440.

Trouw (A) DDB, Amsterdam (CD) Lode Schaeffer/Erik Wünsch
(AD) Lode Schaeffer (CW) Erik Wünsch (P) Boudewijn Smit

As a newspaper, *Trouw* professes to listen to all shades of opinion. No form of expression is inappropriate - however ill-formulated!

**Venture Magazine (A) Pritchard Wood, New York (AD) Neil Costa
(P) Michael Joseph**

The pseudo coup was shot in a London hotel. Its release was
delayed as it was considered to be too threateningly realistic
to run during a particularly turbulent period in South America.

Don't Tell It Magazine (A) Saatchi & Saatchi, London (AD/CW) Jo Tanner/Viv Walsh (Production company) The Dancing Flees

In yer face ads have plugged into attitudes and behaviour already widely displayed in movies and on TV. Yob advertising has taken a pervasive mood of aggression and rebellion into a previously harmless environment. The *Don't Tell It* campaign began with a cinema commercial designed to run with *Pulp Fiction*, *Reservoir Dogs* and the like, before the print ads appeared.

ACKNOWLEDGEMENTS

My thanks to all the outrageously creative creatives whose work appears in this book. And to their PAs, secretaries and agents, as well as the art buyers and account handlers, who helped process the paperwork. Not forgetting the clients who commissioned the work in the first place.

My special thanks also go to Fran, Penny Foulkes, Paul Langham, Bob Prior, Nigel Rawlinson, Tim Rich, Gordon Smith, Philip Spink and Steve Wharton. Thanks, too, to Garry Mouat and Rob Lamb for the design. To Batsford's publicity and sales teams. Martina Stansbie in the editorial department. And, for his editorial discernment, Richard Reynolds, whose brickbats strike harder as the stakes increase.

Calendar for **ABRAFOTO** (Brazilian Photographic Association), Rio de Janeiro (P) Luiz Garrido

Oct 15, 2013

student

$0 .

/22034

Art Center College of Design
Library
1700 Lida Street
Pasadena, Calif. 91103